DANIEL BUINAC

Leaning Walls

Poetry of Falling Frames
Book 2

Globland Books

Published by Globland Books
Copyright © Daniel Buinac 2014

All rights reserved

The right of Daniel Buinac to be identified as the author of this work has been asserted by him in accordance with the Copyright, Designs and Patents Act 1988.

ISBN 978-0-9569634-5-1

Condition of Sale

This book is sold subject to the condition that it shall not by way of trade or otherwise be lent, resold, hired out or otherwise circulated without the publisher's prior consent in any form other than that in which it is published and without a similar condition including this condition being imposed on the subsequent purchaser.

Cover photo by Liis Roden

Contents

Angled Reflections

When Updike Eats an Apple 7
Before Remorse 8
Cutting out the Scene 9
Blindness 10
Presence 11
Molehill 12
Lake 13
Here I Am 14
Suburbia 15
The Beginning and the End 16
Turning Back 17
Hint 18
Today I am Building a Road 19
Until the Justice 20
Sneaking of the 42nd Day 21
Inspiration - Beginnings 22
I Take off Everything 23
Talking about Colours 24
Poem Illustration 25
Man Without a Title 26
Furthermore I am Very Well 27
I Steal Paintings 28
You Will See 29
Breeze Babies 30
I am in Various Stories 31
Poem about Advice that Had no Effect 32
I'll Get Back at You 33
You Pull the Curtains in Panic 34
Only as an Answer... Nothing More... 35
That Wind 36
Let's Build a House 37
Perhaps it's Just a Story 38

I am Not Here 39

Aftertaste

Patch Time 41
Walnut Tree 42
I Know You Entered 43
Some Paintings Attacked Me 44
Silence Has Green Bowels 45
Train 46
With no Understanding 48
Night Between Your and My Body 49
And While 50
About No-exit Doors 51
He is Waiting 52
Tomorrow We'll Dry the River 53
What Now? 54
Through Your Open Window 55
And Not Only That 56
Expectancy 57
Winners 58
I Can't Tell 59
Eyes of a Woman in Love 60
We'll Find a Seashell for Us 61
Hiding 62
But What to Do Really? 63
Memory of an Exhibition 64
Something Worth Sharing 65
I Watch You Drawing 66
Panorama 67
Social Thoughts 68
Sense Disappears Slowly 69
London Tubes 71

Leaning Walls

Angled Reflections

When Updike Eats an Apple

when Updike eats an apple
he does it so extremely thoroughly
at the end regaling equally
with seeds and stem
as with everything else before that

indifferently equally

I fight all
upcoming emptinesses

have you noticed?

Before Remorse

room like high seas, no doors
with eyes, soap scent
and watch still on hand
your back
at the very end of the other half of the bed
sea swallows ship's lights

Cutting out the Scene

when I watched through the window
in direction of the beggar's dog.
before, there was a cinnamon seasoned apple
(gift from your mother) and a summer shower.
after, you will get in with the fat car.
too fast.
water will wake him up.
on the way out,

before the painting falls down,
I learn the sense of smell.

Blindness

with borrowed words
I push air in front of my mouth.
they watch me.
astonished,
they wait in vain.
I go out into smile,
but I dive deep inside myself.
sweaty sunset in their words.
hand on the shoulder…
illusion of consolation
and the strike of reality.
being foreign,
I try to leave.

Presence

no, on the contrary

at the station exit
bus windows turn into
mirrors
whose reflections will blind us
painfully
through the memories

Molehill

open my stomach
when they leave
(when they all leave at last)
and enter with the tongue
of Waring Cuney's woman
with No Images

deep inside
find yourself amongst them all
and face yourself
(leave me)

Lake

Lake
larger than me
we breathe
Thought about depths
is basement of the past
Mud in ears
can't hear your hair

Here I Am

Here I am.
Yesterday we passed each other on the street
with no words.
That won't solve the problem.

I came to talk.
You know, there was a woman after you,
but she had your eyes.
She went with a man who had my eyes.
Perhaps you'll meet him one day
when in your eyes he sees her.
Will you, in his, recognise my eyes?

I came to talk, but this looks like
phone or electricity bill.

I came to talk.
But it's like I already said everything
and it's like you haven't heard anything.

Suburbia

runaway man
dropped his hat.
from a mirror broken by the sun
he is hunted by a wild horse.
spasm and frothy saliva.
in the cocoon serenity
and sticky darkness.
clock.

The Beginning and the End

river listens to the wind.
floating birds make her too tame
and only sudden clouds could save her
from death
in your tear.

Turning Back

when we were buying with farewells,
sewing pockets to the emptiness
so that those left behind
could sneak in their hands
and spend what can't be reached,
but it's warm, ours,
blind for the time
and always behind
(as if not, why would we be
turning back)

Hint

carefully pull out a blue tree
wash your face with earth from the root
cut in a word in the strongest vein
and put the tree back in its place

yesterday in Lisala on the bank
of the Congo river
two women found the heart of a grown-up
male tied with a blue ribbon

in spring listen to leaves
you will get a hint

Today I am Building a Road

today I am building a road
half an hour walk approximately
I'll place it
in Northern Italy
somewhere between Merano and Tirano
will try everything by hand
perhaps even dig a tunnel
buildings are a small concern
but I have a friend - with
an architectural degree
she writes wonderfully

Until the Justice

we marked the border
and removed the earth under our nails
standing each on its own ground.
and we drank.
just as it should be.
when heaven, bitter,
cheered with a thunder
we knew;
paintings would be falling again

Sneaking of the 42nd Day

crushed can
on the way to Holland
(where they smear breasts with margarine)
will leave a mark in the dust

when I find it
between me and your hand
your lips
only time will stand

(if you said so, I too could have
done that)
if rain, 42nd night or wind falls down
(here in Kinshasa all of that
is leaking from my nipples)
I will lose you forever

Inspiration - Beginnings

perhaps even to lose everything
is not enough
like when I started drawing I used to draw
silhouettes of people
and not people
some ruins are…

I Take off Everything

and walk the foreign streets naked
dividing them in half
using odd criterion of curtains
and I'm not scared of sympathy
inside the bus
in which they dress me
breakfast hanging from their mouths
their eyes full of my nudity

Talking about Colours

talking about colours
I know
when I finally use darkness
to wash them off
I will hear her
"Only now?"

and later I won't know
what I am supposed to do
when the day irreversibly dawns

Poem Illustration

I come every day
I eat dried waves of
potato juice
exchanged for three sketched strophes
and I tremble

their fat ears are licking the words
they call it blues
(they are hungry for my hunger)

Man Without a Title

is buying a drink to a fat-eyebrow lady
at the bottom of my new restaurant
doesn't matter for the cigarette ashes
wrinkled tie
broken glass under the table
or posh guests with watchful eyes
doesn't matter that he is buying drink
to my wife
nor that she didn't say no
doesn't matter about the hands
or her loud laughter
his title is not important either
because if important to me
it would then be important to her too

however it is completely unacceptable
to get out of the house (my house)
with untamed eyebrows
(Miss Tiberi didn't have a day off)

Furthermore I am Very Well

Furthermore I am very well
and I expect that soon

only in shirt,
with acceptance-watch on tongue
and coast of spread arms

you come by and say
It's me

I Steal Paintings

I steal paintings from passers-by eyes
empty canvasses or started sketches
I sew sail from canvasses
I make wind from sketches
and I keep going
my sources are plentiful
my decisions are effortless

You Will See

You will see
when the lights go down
You will know
when the drank stage and all these
strange people cool down
To whom
and about whom you sing

Breeze Babies

bridges that even
winds don't dare
to cross

are now part of
with morning wine-washed
loft, arranged table
and warm bedding

where in between their
weak pillars flow
torrents of verses, looks and touches
playing with the very existence
of ever more tired structures that
straddle them

however
certain winds like
exactly those kinds of bridges

I am in Various Stories

I am in various stories
loads of bad paper
smell of printed metal
dust wads
wind is throwing words around
fingers are changing their meaning

only the bill stays the same

Poem about Advice that Had no Effect

When you tame a big river
you watch two things;
your head and her dignity

Today we ate News at Ten

I'll Get Back at You

I'll get back at you for this absence!
I'll beat you up when I see you…
I'll torture you with tickling…
I'll whisper in your ear
until the lust drains you…
I'll kiss you until you cry…
I'll eat all your fingers…
Steal all your alpha states…
Drain that source of yours…
I'll make you draw with waterproof markers
on your stomach…
I'll forbid any food…
I'll walk naked around the flat…
At the end I'll drive you crazy by begging
for forgiveness with my tears…
So it's up to you now…

You Pull the Curtains in Panic

you pull the curtains in panic
you don't even peek

I see your vein spasm on hands
I see your frosted sweat on skin
I see your lips shake
I see your restless breath
I see your eyelids - guards
that build a wall to desirous eyes

I see your naked thoughts

Only as an Answer... Nothing More...

truth about size
(in the August night full of shivering)
torn off button
(you said it was small)
starts to be clear the very moment
when you try to put it back into place
while still attached to the heart
by the thoughts of my hands
on your dress

disproportion with its own
buttonhole
will make you ask yourself surprised
where am I
and why am I not next to you

That Wind

that wind of ours
lashed with willow branches
tormented, scared
of noises that it itself creates

that dress
since a couple of moments ago
without a button
hidden in the grass under the bench

that carousel of yours
and scummed mouth of a horse
on the cloud above us

Let's Build a House

let's build a house
with walls of coloured pebbles
from some childhood river,
with windows in Gibraltar
and Siberian snow on the roof

let's build the house
with verse carpets
and chandeliers of tiny, glimmering
paintings that chime at a touch of breath

let's build into the house
all our whisperings
and looks,
all voyages to Neptune,
all intangible pottery sculptured
by interlaced hands,
all escaped smiling thoughts,
salt, vine,
icons and incense

let's build the house
because of the house itself,
take each other's hand
and leave,
turning back occasionally
with nostalgia

Perhaps it's Just a Story

a friend tells me
before splashing paint on the finished painting

I am Not Here

I am not here.
at least for some time.
some longer time.
some time between or before.
definitely not after.

Aftertaste

Patch Time

oh it's a patch time
couple of holes here and there
should be fine
should cover pride
should serve for a while

Walnut Tree

I'll write to you about my plan
to plant a walnut tree
there's a huge park behind my place
they say some gentleman a long time ago
gifted it to the council so that
the public can enjoy
ten football grounds would fit at least
trees who knows how old
three men couldn't join their
hands around them

but no walnut tree

and I keep thinking if there was only one

perhaps I shall secretly plant it overnight
but what when they cut the grass
they will cut it down too
maybe I should try
under the shadow of a bigger tree
and move it when it matures
but how would it grow without sunlight

I'll see think about it will write to you
although perhaps I have no rights

but I would so like to write to you
there are lots of things
not just the walnut tree

I Know You Entered

I know you entered.
I don't move.
I don't breathe.

Slowly
carefully
you wander the most distant corners
to you always and again
insufficiently known space around me.

I feel
I count with beats
your impatience
your innocent ritual
of arousing the stage fright.

Senses on a pottery wheel
silence
breath on the skin
vortex.

Then steppe, steppe, steppe
then stars.

Some Paintings Attacked Me

some paintings attacked me
sounds
smells
years ago pushed somewhere into the guts
and now they appear just like that,
as if I don't care

not sure if I should fight
or how one is actually supposed to fight...

I close my eyes while driving

Silence Has Green Bowels

silence has green bowels
and on them slow eyes with no irises

what is left when you learn silence?

Don't go,
it will rain,
can't you hear?

Train

Sitting on a train
staring at the shoes
swallowed by the noise
And stubbed
by the rhythm of the move

I know that fog is around me
I know that winter is on its way
And I know there is
nothing in the window
No smile or pain
Only fields

So I look at you in the past

Paper bag and superstore
Swimsuit and sunglasses
Messed up hair and morning eyes
Shiny shoes and lipstick match
Live music restaurant
Half-smile and touch of hands
Sunday market, handmade stuff
Nice building photograph

And me me me by your side

And look at you now
All alone in the dark
All the chairs are monsters

When you turn off the light

and you're hurting the remote control
Still your eyes look aside
through the shaky shadows
Wide
to the train running through the fields

Call me call me
Call me and I'll run
Through the smoky sky
and the rainy forests
of the past

And I know there is
nothing in the window
No smile or pain
Only fields

With no Understanding

with my coat carelessly draped
over all moments of sleepless night
and with raised, sober, morning mist collar
at the underground station
on the floor of the unknown room
in a constellation behind Ireland and Australia
next to the Thames
I follow how

with extinguishing thoughts on common
portions of just bloomed madness

with blurry melancholy, but decidedly

she steps out maybe forever
from my clean, naive and unreal train car
in the smog of everyday
carrying me like a child's herbarium
in the corner of a completely new smile
which others will notice
with excitement, astonishment or envy
but with no understanding

Night Between Your and My Body

night between your and my body

defiant sigh is a lightning
that slits the distance

And While

and while you look
somewhere far away through me
down our misted glass a drop will get going

About No-exit Doors

slipped through my fingers
train with a hundred and eighty passengers.

I turn to my father;
unspoken pain and anguish on his face.
in a moment I'm devoured by nothingness.

in the moment
that will for sure last forever

as this time
I failed to wake up.

He is Waiting

He is waiting.
He didn't take the first table
next to the window,
she would spot him.
Does he want that?
Yesterday he was sitting just like this.
Someone who looks like her passed on
the other side of the street.
Blood
Left his body
Dripping through his fingers
Clenched around
southern-fried chicken
In the integral bread.
He didn't exist until she disappeared.
Her hands, body moves, whispers
Everything came back, taste of nipples
promises
What if she comes again today,
what if that wasn't her,

what if it was, what if she doesn't come?
He leaves the table to pay,
returns the plate, walks out

His life suddenly has a meaning.

Tomorrow We'll Dry the River

tomorrow we'll dry the river

all heads down
all hands hidden
not looking at each other

when I get home
I'll take a paintbrush
and until tomorrow I'll paint
without touching the canvas

in the riverbed mud
stars

What Now?

I had a good thought
and deep in myself
I exchanged heavy words
and I offended myself several times
separated from myself
and reconciled
without saying a word to myself
aloud
and shouted and cried
waved my hands in anger
and frowned
then smiled with melancholy
and held myself in a tight
hug
whispered comfort and pouted
and then sat down hugged
and watched some romantic
comedy
angry that I let it go
to myself again so easily

if it happens again
I promise it will be the last time
I promise that I won't pull out
and will stick
to the decision that I cannot
live like this with myself any more

Through Your Open Window

through your open window
in Moscow
on my spread canvasses
in an empty London room
morning snow
has fallen,
drop of milk
and breakfast
breadcrumbs

I'll wait for some time
on the bedding smell

And Not Only That

and not only that
sometimes they are hollow
and don't smell at all
where the road ends
they disappear forgotten
in the darkness of someone's pocket

why are you calling them stars?

Expectancy

so when you wish
with your shaky fingers,
taken by disbelief and passion,
to touch the flaky, white layer of time
on substantively black lacquer
of our piano

remembering
with your sophisticated beauty
the colossal melodies
that we composed on it with such ease
with our vulnerably sensual
bodies

you should know
that it awaits you
steadily
in my eyes

Winners

You who I meet on streets
You whose needles are in my eyes
who laugh so loud when nothing is funny
You who put cream on your elbows
so you can use them better in offices, buses
or beds
You whose daughters suck off celebrities
who are sympathetic to their wickedness
You who don't know about God
You who are All
who are unavoidable
who steal this world without shame
You gents have won
and I congratulate You on that
with all the disgust that
I can express with tired and drained words
You, gents, are the winners

I Can't Tell

I can't tell for how long
I've been watching walls of the tube
Around me they read, listen, talk
We don't share the space
If we don't notice each other

Without any particular expression on our faces
we desperately fight for the air
Stuffy and heavy
At the same time
I fight not to inhale too much of it

Eyes of a Woman in Love

eyes of a woman in love
she sits across
at the cedar table and smokes

her face full of moonlight
her hands blue with inability
to hide feelings
she is watching him
I am watching her

We'll Find a Seashell for Us

we'll find a seashell for us

abandoned, empty,
with wrinkles made by human hands,
patient in its silence

we'll wash it with clear warm
movements of words,
inhale the sound of the gulf into it
and disappear in its depths

with the first stronger wave
it will be good to us

Hiding

some things started to walk behind me
queue
to draw attention
I act some things are following me
and I turn back from time to time
they stop
in shop windows their true faces
nonchalant and patient
when I start walking they smile gently
pityingly
that's not naive at all
some things will grow up like that

But What to Do Really?

it's not enough to look down the street.
not to change face
while they talk.
not to talk back while they change
faces.
while they walk away.
wave with hands.
forget.

Memory of an Exhibition

while distance was recognising me
by wiping the details away,
by oblivion
and impossibility of touch,
women without nipples
under the dying light of dried colours
that makes wrinkles
cried,
framed and motionlessly
faithful to the canvas,
with the tears of the foreigner
that I was

Something Worth Sharing

thought about leaving the title only
would I be understood?
train stopped on the bridge
(small babbling stream)
not in a hurry any more
(Turner-like, much older)

I Watch You Drawing

I watch you drawing
lips on the misted window

roofs are clean after rain

let's not think
about the last night
let me tell you
about dolphins and their
world of blue
let me talk to you
about anything
just move your thoughts away
just come back to this moment
just look me in the eyes
and feel

I will read
and I'll know when you are mine again

Panorama

streets end in wind
clouds stickily
descend to the sea
scars on the stone
watery dust
(brings someone's laugh)
(tourists)
(from Italy)
(camera)
(play)
needle
pain

Social Thoughts

didn't think that crowd would matter
didn't care
so when they spoke and
were taken seriously
I was not only confused,
but lost,
said the painter.
I can see it
even on the small format
in The 20th Century Art Book,
pocket edition.

Sense Disappears Slowly

She sits across from me.
I watch as she puts on make-up
In the half-empty train.

Why are you doing that?
World is not worthy of you.

Our eyes don't meet.
She checks her phone
Takes chocolate
Sips from the water bottle
Puts in eye drops
Stands up
Opens the window

Cold wind squeezes my tears out

Carefully,
but skillfully
she climbs into the window frame
Then she Turns
and while her half-smile is saying:
    I understand
She straightens
Fixes her coat
Positions the handbag
Spreads her arms

And throws herself

In a torrent of pictures
of the world that Unstoppably gallops

And before I manage to make a move
Jump
Turn
She is raising above
the blackberry bush
with powerful beating of wings

The pupils of her made-up
eyes
Soak up the sky

London Tubes

only once we've finished
with digging
I realised
that we are guilty
for some winds will be born
live out their lives and die
never getting out
of Earth's womb

www.ingramcontent.com/pod-product-compliance
Lightning Source LLC
Chambersburg PA
CBHW020627300426
44112CB00010B/1230